COMING
OUT
ASIAN

Reflections on identity, acceptance and living
authentically for LGBT Asians

Mun Wye Chng & John Rozzelle

Dedication

This book is the product of a long gestation period that took place across continents, and many long conversations between us. It is in part a record of our growing relationship but also our contribution to the world at large, one that we hope will play some small part in helping make life better for someone out there experiencing the kind of doubt and uncertainty that we ourselves have faced in living life in the closet.

We need to thank several people who helped proofread, comment and critique our book as it made its way to its final form, as well as those who gave this book its inspiration, or contributed their personal insights to the coming out process based on their own experiences.

Our thanks to Eugene and Stan for their insightful and very useful feedback on the draft, as well as sharing their lives and their stories with us. The "Asian Mafia" for starting it all for us in Fort Lauderdale, and then providing even more encouragement and inspiration as time went on – know that you are our home away from home always. To Wan, the best sister (and sister-in-law) one could ask for, and a great sounding board for all our ideas. Thank you for supporting us and giving us the benefit of your intellect, insight and experience.

Preface

The epiphany happened over dinner one balmy night in Miami. My partner John and I had been invited over to a friend's house for a housewarming hotpot dinner. There were six of us altogether. Bo and Sam, who were from China, Hong and Joseph, who were from the Philippines, me (from Singapore) and John, who was the only American at the table. We were treated to an awesome Shanghai-style hotpot, with mountains of sliced beef, pork, chicken, and not to mention a ton of vegetables. There was also quite a lot of wine and cocktails on the table that night.

At some point during that dinner, the conversation turned to Bo's parents who were coming to visit from China. Someone — I don't remember who — asked him if his parents knew that he was gay. This wasn't a surprising question, because all the men at this dinner were either bi or gay. All the Asians were my friends from a gay men's group. Hong teased Bo, asking him if he would like us all to go to the airport, welcome his parents to the US and introduce them to all our gay friends. Unsurprisingly, Bo demurred, and flipped the question back to Hong – do *your* parents know that you're gay?

"I think so," was Hong's reply, but he confessed he had never told them – he only thought that they would have guessed by now, because he had been single for so many years and never brought a girl home. There was a bit more good-natured ribbing, going around the table asking each other if we had come out to our families. Bo defended himself, saying that it was particularly hard for him to come out to his parents because they were Chinese. He turned to me and said, "You know what I mean right? Asian parents, enough said!".

It was sometime after the dinner while we were driving home, that John turned to me in the car and remarked, "Did you realize something at dinner? There were five of you around that table, all gay Asian men living a long way from your families back home, and you were the only one who was out to your family!" And it was true. Strangely enough, even though all of my friends were highly accomplished in their own fields and were living comfortably gay lives in various degrees of openness in the US, some with boyfriends and even husbands, none of them had told their families that they were gay, or that they had male partners.

And so, we began to wonder, why is it that so few gay Asian men come out to their families? Is it because Asian culture and society are simply so conservative and family-oriented that it makes it nearly impossible to do so? Is it due to a fear of bringing deep shame on family and ancestors? Is it because Asian men simply don't feel the desire to come out? Is it because they don't know if, when or how to come out?

Most of our gay friends, both Asian and Western, tell us they wish they could come out, if they have not already done so. Wanting to live truthfully, honestly and authentically is a universal human desire. So maybe it really isn't that Asian men *don't* want to come out. Perhaps it's that it's simply hard to do so, because unlike in Western societies, our families tend not to talk about issues of the heart. We may not even know how to talk frankly about any aspect of our personal lives, much less about being gay or lesbian, because we don't have the experience or even the words to do so.

This book is our attempt to change this.

A Few Words About "Asians"

The term "Asian" is very broad, as Asia is a huge continent that includes many diverse cultures, religions, and ethnicities. "Coming Out Asian" is written from the perspective of a Chinese Singaporean, but many other cultures, including the Chinese, Japanese, Korean, and Vietnamese share a similar strong Confucian influence. Similarly, cultures termed East Asian and South Asian, while diverse in their religious beliefs, histories, and customs, share many of the same familial and societal pressures in being an LGBTQ person and coming out as such. For the sake of conciseness, we have used the word "Asian" to refer to these shared experiences across cultures.

Likewise, the word "gay" is used throughout this book as a representation for the broader LGBTQ community. We use it primarily to be concise, but also because it is rooted in our personal narratives and experiences. It is meant to address our collective shared experiences, and we sincerely hope and believe that the information presented in this book will offer value, insight, and support to the wider LGBTQ community.

Table of Contents

Introduction

The process of coming out can be complicated for anyone, but for Asians it can be especially difficult. Cultural pressures like "filial piety," family honour, saving face, parental shame, the importance of family lineage/dynasty, and the expectation to conform to "traditional" norms and values can be huge obstacles in the coming out process.

Coming Out Asian addresses each of these. It is for people who are curious about coming out, who are thinking about coming out, in the process of coming out or actively making a plan to come out. It is about identifying blocks — within ourselves, our families and society — and working through each of them. It is a book to help with self-reflection and how to know if you're ready to come out, how to know if others are ready for you to come out to them, and how to create a safe plan for each. Most importantly, this book is an exercise in learning to love ourselves, to build an authentic life and to celebrate who we truly are and were born to be. It will prepare you to navigate the often-difficult road to authenticity.

Coming out is not a one-time event; rather, it's a process, one that repeats itself with each person we come out to. It is a challenging, complex, and deeply personal decision to make, one that takes courage and proper planning to execute. It must be done on your terms and only when you are sure you're ready.

So, congratulations on picking up this book. Life is better lived openly and authentically without hiding in the shadows. Ask almost anyone who *has* come out and they will tell you how much better their life is after doing so.

Let's get started!

Our Coming Out Stories

On the drive home that night after dinner ...

J: "That was fun. It's good to see everybody."

MW: "Indeed, it was. And that hot pot was amazing. Bo outdoes himself every time.

J: "I know! What a spread! Tons of everything and the broth was perfect. Not too *mala* for a white guy ...

MW: "And the renovations look great. The house is really coming along. It'll be quite the place when it's finished."

J: "Hey, can I ask you something?

MW: "Seriously, John?? We just renovated a year ago!"

J: "No, not that. But, come to think of it, it *has* been a whole year...

MW: Ugh.

JR: No, what I wanted to ask was, there were five Asian men at the table tonight, all gay, all successful professionals, and you're the only one who's out. Why is that?"

MW: "Well I can think of a few reasons, but I'll bet the main one is they're all from Asian families. I know it sounds cliche to state that Asian family dynamics are quite different from Western ones, but it can't be understated how much Confucian values play a role in shaping how people think about hard questions like being open about their sexuality. I can't speak for all Asians, but Chinese men are socialized from birth that the most important duty they have in life is to continue the family line, and it is in service of honouring their parents and ancestors that they are required to do this. Basically, your only "true" duty in life is to bear sons, so that your family name can live on and on. That was pretty clear to me growing up, when it was pointed out to me from the age of maybe 9 or 10, that I was "precious" because I was the only grandson bearing the family name."

J: "I think you're precious for *many* reasons ... "

MW: "Of course you do, darling, but as I was saying, this "Filial piety" is probably the biggest contributing stress factor that gay Asians (sons, in particular) face when thinking about coming out, because it embodies all three of the important aspects of Confucian values — hierarchy, harmony and face. Confucian societies emphasize the maintenance of harmony at all levels of society in order for the society (or country) to grow and prosper. Harmony is maintained through "proper" behaviours in hierarchical relationships (ruler–subject, parent–child, husband–wife etc), and is kept in balance with 'face' ".

J: "Right. And what's *that* about?"

MW: "Basically, it's not to embarrass yourself or others. Generally speaking, you have to give other people face (and other people are supposed to give you face), and you're not supposed to behave in an embarrassing manner (thus throwing away your precious face). If everyone does their part, then everyone is happy and the world goes merrily on its way. But if you cause someone to lose face? Well then, we've got problems. Sometimes BIG problems. So you can imagine that going against the grain by coming out and being open about your sexuality, many parents may see it as you throwing away your face and in turn *their face* as well ("All your family is disgrace!" as the saying goes). This causes a cascading loss of face that can be irreparable in some cases. Just thinking about the consequences could make someone very afraid to come out, indeed.

J: Okay, but all that said, why did *you* come out?"

MW: "I'll tell you a crazy story, something that stuck with me for a long while. Years ago, while on holiday, I went to a palm reading on a whim. The fortune teller looked at my palm, then at me, and said that I had two life lines. He hesitated for just a split second before saying that it meant I would always be safe because I have a "backup" literally, a "lifeline". I told this to a good friend who was a family therapist and also gay, and with whom I had shared a little bit about my confusion about my sexuality in the past. He remarked half-jokingly that maybe the two life lines meant I was living a double / parallel life. I knew it was a jest, and I don't put much stock in palm reading in terms of predicting the future, but in that moment, I knew there was a kernel of truth in that jest, and the hesitation I'd detected in the fortune teller's voice could very well have been just me recognizing the fact that I was indeed living a double life. I ruminated on that experience for a long while. Eventually, I felt something inside compelling me to share the truth with my loved ones in the hope that we could have a more authentic relationship without my having to expend more energy living a double life."

J: "So, for you it was about honesty?"

MW: "Yes, and I was really getting tired of trying to hide things from the people that I loved. But you know, I didn't come out to my immediate family until just before we met, when I was 35. Coming out wasn't something that I had thought about for years. In fact, in my twenties I was totally convinced that I would never let my family know that I was gay and I was willing to make excuses and pretend for as long as I could, and hopefully take my secret to the grave with me. I think a lot of gay folks in Asia grew up thinking that, and I know people who still do. But I guess with age and the passing of time it just got harder and harder to keep things separate, and I've never really felt the need to keep anything else about my life from my loved ones. Maybe I'm a bit of an oversharer. So this one big secret was getting too much to keep. And maybe I was naive but I thought that because my parents always told me not to lie and not to keep secrets from them, that if I came out to them, they would see that I was trying to be a good son by having as authentic and honest a relationship with them as I could.

J: Right.

MW: But I knew it was going to be difficult because gay wasn't a "thing" in my family, culture or country.

J: Is that what your parents thought when you came out to them? That you couldn't be gay because there are no gay people in Singapore?

MW: Well, no, it wasn't quite so simplistic or dramatic, but I guess in some way my parents' reaction was a product of what they were exposed to or not exposed to, to be precise. When I came out to my parents over video call, I remember that they were initially confused as to what I was telling them. At first I told them I was "gay" and they seemed not to understand what I meant, so I had to elaborate and say that I was attracted to men and not women. That took a while to sink in and they were quite shocked for a couple of days. When we spoke again a few days later they were in denial. My mom didn't know what to make of it, and my dad kept asking if it was something that could be "cured".

 I was really nervous before I told them, but once the words had left my mouth, it became much easier. I was surprised, and my sis told me later she was too, how calm and reassuring I seemed when I came out to my parents. The first few conversations that I had with them about coming out, I don't think I even shed a tear while we were talking, even when my mum started crying. I think you kind of get into this "counselling" mode when you take the step to come out (or at least I did). Maybe each of us has a different way of responding, and it probably also varies depending on where you are in your life at the point when you come out.

Going back to what we talked about earlier — it's not just that Asian families with Confucian values make it harder for sons to come out to their parents. As much as it's a stereotype, it's also very true that most Asian families don't talk about feelings and emotional needs. Part of it is cultural — we don't really have the language to have conversations about our feelings. Yes of course we have words to describe how we feel, but the idea of talking things out in order to sort out emotional needs is quite an alien concept in most Asian families. This means most Asian parents are not experienced in handling conversations about emotional and psychological issues, hence it often falls to the children to try and facilitate any conversation. This makes it extra challenging for anyone who is an only child, who may not have the benefit of a supportive sibling to help facilitate these conversations.

J: So you think it's important for kids to approach the subject with parents and guide them through, because many parents wouldn't have a clue how to do it themselves?

MW: Basically, yes, because of the nature of the conversation. It's an emotional topic that requires certain vocabulary. In addition, parents of a certain age bracket might have no clear idea about what gay/LGBT people or lives are about. Some parents might associate homosexuality only with the danger of AIDS, because that was the only information they were exposed to in the mainstream media during the 1980s and 90s. In some countries like Singapore, where there is a strong governmental control over the media, this is made more difficult because positive portrayals of LGBT people are banned on books and TV. Without positive role models in the media, both LGBT people and their parents have less exposure to what it really means to live as a healthy, well-adjusted and open person.

You are probably very aware that the love language of most Asian parents is through providing material comfort, especially through food! Do your parents or relatives express their love through feeding you?

J: Eh, we had six kids in my family. Food was more about survival. Grab it before it's gone.

MW: Is that why you eat so fast?

J: And your original point was ...?

MW: That many Asian children learn to associate comfort with love, until they come up against something that forces them to re-evaluate this. And in many cases this might only happen when the child is already an adult and has their own life. We might only realize later in life that comfort does not equate to love, that providing comfort, while necessary for the welfare of a child, is not sufficient for the complete and balanced development of the child into an adult. Love is more than just making sure material needs are met, or soothing a hurt or injury. We often avoid talking about "difficult" subjects because it feels uncomfortable, so in avoiding the conversation, we remain "comfortable", but the underlying problem still persists.

J: So are there any tips for talking to Asian parents?

MW: I think it's the same as the rest of life. We all have times when we have to have difficult conversations — medical issues, relationship issues, job interviews, managing staff, asking the boss for a raise. Coming out is the same. You think carefully about what you're going to say, you make a plan of how, when and where to do it, you rehearse it a thousand times, and then you have the conversation. It's important, however, to be mindful that people may stumble and be at a loss while they're searching for the right language to use at the same time they're processing feelings.

J: And you said your reason for coming out was to be honest, because your parents told you to never keep secrets from them?

MW: Well, yes. That and …

J: How'd it go?

MW: It's complicated. As you know, it's STILL complicated. But to answer your question, I came out to my parents on a video call, as I was living in the US at the time. There was a lot of confusion. When I said, "I want you to know I'm gay," they seemed not to understand what I meant. I had to elaborate and say that I was attracted to men and not women.

J: Maybe that cultural lack of language thing?

MW: I think so. They were just dumbfounded. There was silence and a lot of stumbling, searching for words, like it was just too much for them to wrap their heads around. I'm very grateful to my sister for being there both for my moral support and to help mediate and explain things to my parents when I told them. But even then, it was so awkward; we just ended the call because they asked for time to process the news.

When we spoke again a few days later they were in denial. My mom didn't know what to make of it, and my dad kept asking if it was something that could be "cured". My mom eventually started getting emotional, crying spontaneously when she thought about me, losing sleep and not eating well, basically being depressed. My dad didn't know how to handle that and asking him to take her to see a therapist or psychiatrist was a dead end because of the stigma that they had about mental health (only "crazy" people need that kind of help). In fact, my dad countered by saying that maybe I was the one who needed to see a psychiatrist.

Perhaps if I had been right there by their side, we could have had better conversations and I might have been able to convince my mom to go to family therapy with me on the pretext that I did indeed need counselling (which I probably did, in fact). It took them a couple of months to get over the initial shock of the revelation and let their emotions settle a bit.

The good thing was they were already scheduled to fly to the US to spend the summer with me in a couple of months after I came out to them. So I spent three months living with them again, trying to show them that I was still me, still the son they've always known and loved, only now they knew one more thing about me that they didn't know before. It was good for us to have that experience. We travelled around the US and even went on a cruise together.

Sometimes my mom would think about my sexuality and get emotional again and I would have to explain to her that it was nothing to be worried about, but she still worried that life would be hard for me (if people found out).

After they'd spent a couple of months living with me in the US and traveling around, they came to accept that my sexuality wasn't something changeable and that it was just what it was, something that we would all have to live with.

But they settled on a second line of "mental defence" which was basically to ask me not to act on my sexuality, or at least not let them know. They didn't want me to date someone, or at least not bring any man home to meet them. The first was a promise I couldn't make to them, as I was already looking online and dating at the time when they told me this, and I wasn't going to stop.

J: Uh, wait a minute ...

MW: The second was not a promise I made to them either, because I hoped that someday they would be ok with me bringing a man home with me and I told them that I would hold out for that day so I wouldn't promise to never do that. So we were left at an impasse.

J: — Indeed.

MW: I was really nervous before I told them, but once the words had left my mouth, it became much easier. I was surprised, and my sis told me later she was too, how calm and reassuring I seemed when I came out to my parents. The first few conversations that I had with them about coming out, I don't think I even shed a tear while we were talking, even when my mum started crying. I think you kind of get into this "counselling" mode when you take the step to come out (or at least I did). Maybe each of us has a different way of responding, and it probably also varies depending on where you are in your life at the point when you come out.

J: I think that's right — the quality of the relationship, everyone's familiarity with the subject matter, how ready someone is to come out — definitely all dynamics that affect how the conversation will go. But it's important to remember that the person coming out drives the conversation and ultimately is in control of it. We can never predict how people will respond to what we're saying, but we can control how we respond in kind.

MW: And so why did you come out?
J: "Same thing, really. It was about honesty, authenticity and trying to build and deepen familial bonds. I think you know this part of the story, but I had met a guy — coincidentally, also an Asian guy —

while traveling on a business trip. We carried on a long-distance relationship for about a year, meeting in cities around the US, as we both travelled frequently for work. He'd met my family, but they didn't know who he was other than a friend. As our relationship deepened, I wanted to incorporate him into the family. I wanted them to know who he was, who I was, and who we were. I wanted to live openly and authentically, with dignity and respect, and I knew the only way that was going to happen was for me to come out. But making the decision and mustering the courage to do so was a long, arduous process.

MW: "Well, good thing you dumped him or you'd have never met me"

J: "I didn't dump him, not really. We were together for three years, but couldn't really grow as a couple — not in the traditional sense, anyway. He wasn't out to his family, and kept us and our families separated. It's that double life thing. It's also one of the great ironies of my life: to come out to my family to bring him in, but not have it reciprocated. The relationship was doomed to fail. The energy invested into keeping secrets would have been far better spent building the bonds required for a healthy, mature relationship.

MW: Wait, so you came out to your mom because you wanted to introduce him to her as your partner?

J: Yeah…

MW: Had you not come out before because you weren't in a relationship or because you didn't even know you were bisexual?

J: Oh, I knew I was, but they didn't. They'd met my serious girlfriends over the years and assumed I was straight.
MW: Either way, it sounds like a romantic gesture on your part. But did you discuss it with him before you decided to come out to your family? Did he agree to do the same and then renege on his promise? Or did you feel that integrating him with your family was so important that you went ahead and did it for yourself regardless and just hoped that he would do the same?

J: So many questions, so little time ...

MW: *Whatever.*

J: Honestly, a few of my family members were planning a week-long trip and I wanted to include him. We'd been dating for about a year, talking a lot about building a future together, the relationship was serious. To me, the logical, adult thing to do was to come out, to let my family know who *we* were, and to have him accepted into the family. It was a risk, but one I thought was worth it.

MW: And...?

JR: I was insanely nervous. I'd thought it over for days, weighing the risk and the sheer gravity of the situation. Based on what I knew from life experience and my psychology and social work training, it was clear that we could never have a deep, meaningful and sustainable relationship — one that bound us and our families together if I didn't.

MW: You mean, like straight couples?

JR. Exactly. And I knew I had to come out to them in order to make that happen. I mean, straight, gay, whatever, how do you form a deep emotional bond with someone (including extended family) when you're keeping secrets from them? When they don't really know who you are?

MW: I agree completely. So what did you do?

JR: It was Mother's Day. I took her some flowers and we were just chatting. I hadn't planned on telling her then, exactly, but I HAD planned on the possibility that after telling her she may not ever want to speak to me again.

MW: Ugh. Yeah.

J: Well, the conversation turned to the pending trip. It seemed the time was right, so I told her.

MW: And ...?

JR: And she didn't believe me.

MW: *Wha...?*

JR: Seriously. I had to tell her three times, really sell her on it. She kept saying, "Gay? You? ..No, you can't be." The problem she was having wasn't my *being* gay, it was that her masculine-appearing son didn't look like the effeminate images of gays she'd seen portrayed in the American media.

MW: Oh, right. And she was okay with it?

JR: Yeah, I'm lucky. She said, "You're my son. I love you no matter what." Then she called all her friends and outed me to them, one by one.

MW: Did she?

JR: Yeah, I'm not sure why. I had every right to be upset by that, but I didn't mind, really. She had a very juicy piece of news that might put her in the spotlight for a while amongst her friends. In telling them about me, she was kind of outing herself as well as the parent of a gay kid.

MW: Well, we all have our different, very personal reasons for coming out, don't we?

JR: Indeed, we do ...

In our core, most of us have the desire to come out of the closet. Our reasons for doing so might vary from person to person, but there is a common theme shared by most of us. We want to live authentically, be ourselves in the open, and have people love us for who we are, not who we pretend to be. As you read below, try to think of your own situation. Knowing why you want to come out is an important first step in the process.

A Few Reasons to Come Out

Authenticity — When we are in the closet, we present a version of ourselves to others that is not who we really are, but who we think others want us to be. We often live with the fear that if people know who we REALLY are, they will reject and ridicule us (or worse). This uncertainty creates internal anxiety, and in the long term, can damage self-esteem. Coming out allows us to fully be ourselves and have others love and accept us for being us, not who they think we are. And as we build authentic friendships and community based on this acceptance, we begin to love and trust ourselves more.

Secrets vs. Honesty — Science has proven that keeping secrets can be very bad for our health by creating an "anxiety loop." An anxiety loop works like this: Keeping a secret creates anxiety, and the more nervous we are about it being found out, the more anxiety it creates. Coming out eliminates what for most of us is our deepest and longest held secret. It eliminates the constant fear of being "found out," and all the stress, guilt and shame that goes along with it. Nearly everyone who comes out reports feelings of freedom, of honesty, of a better sense of Self. These feelings of "lightness" and "relief" come from shedding the mental and emotional weight of keeping the secret buried, and constantly worrying whether it will be somehow revealed.

Build Deeper Emotional Bonds — For gay people, dating is an evolutionary process. Many of us start with shadowy, anonymous hook-ups, eventually grow to the point of actually spending time together with someone in public. But even after we've reached that milestone, there's always a fear of getting found out to be something more than friends. "Are we sitting too close?" Are we laughing too much? Will the waiter notice we're gazing into each other's eyes? We're often on guard against being discovered as lovers, subconsciously balancing love and commitment with the fear of being found out. This can unintentionally keep us at an emotional distance, sabotaging our ability to fully give of ourselves in a relationship.

But when you're out, laughing too much and giving each other attention are no longer worries; rather, they are signs of a good relationship, one that will make others jealous. Simply put, dating becomes easier when we don't have to hide what we're doing. (Hook-ups do too!). But more than just dating, being out allows us to commit fully to someone else, without fear or creating a world of secrecy. Imagine any straight married couple you know. Now imagine if no one knew about the wife — not parents, friends, family, co-workers, neighbours, no one. Nothing could be shared about her, not moments of joy or sorrow, not difficulties in the relationship, not where you went on vacation, what you did on the weekend, what she cooked for dinner last night, nothing. And now imagine how the wife would feel, being kept hidden from the world. Coming out of the closet lifts the veil of secrecy around dating and relationships, elevating them to a place of honour and dignity they deserve. It allows us to give fully of ourselves to our partners (and their families, if we so choose) to create deep, lasting, familial bonds. It is said that honesty is the cornerstone of any successful relationship. Having an "out" relationship puts that cornerstone firmly in place.

To normalize ourselves – Do you know someone who is "other"? A foreigner, maybe? Someone of different race, religion, culture, intelligence, or socio-economic status? Have you ever tried to "put people in boxes," saying "these people are like this" or "all _____ people are _____? We often discriminate or stereotype people because we don't really know them. But those misconceptions usually fade away once we start spending time with people and become familiar with them. In fact, social scientists have proved that when people know others of a different race, religion or nationality, they are much less likely to be racist or to tolerate racism or religious bias in their presence.

When we're in the closet, people THINK they know us. But

when we come out to them, we show them our true Selves. We show them that gay people are just like everyone else, that we're all the things they loved in us before we came out. As important as Gay Pride parades have been around the world in fostering awareness of the LGBTQ community, they may have had unintended consequences. The camp fun and outrageousness of men in thongs, in drag, and in various other states of dress/undress presented only one aspect of the gay community. People who don't directly know anyone who's LGBTQ may think that ALL gay people wear rainbow jock straps and ride around on floats all day. While nowhere near as exciting or dramatic, Pride parades might do well by featuring people dressed in business suits or military uniforms, or as doctors, nurses, teachers, plumbers, truck drivers, farmers or any other average person in society. If so, people may begin to see LGBTQ people as being as normal as the person next door.

In the meantime, there's you. Coming out can normalize you in the eyes of loved ones and can dispel myths about the LGBTQ community. (Unless of course you only wear rainbow jock straps and ride around on floats all day…). And, as social scientists know, when straight people know a gay person, they're far less apt to be homophobic or to tolerate homophobia in their presence.

Help empower others – We start out alone, just us and our secret. No one to turn to - to share our feelings with, to help us navigate life, to help us defend against ridicule, to tell us everything will be alright, to show what is possible now and in the future. Our lives are filled with role models, often of the hero archetype: an athlete, a movie star, or a successful businessperson. But role models are more often found closer to home: parents, relatives, teachers, and community leaders. These are people we look to for guidance, for strength, for inspiration, for a way forward.

What happens when you don't have a role model? Many LGBTQ people don't. We might look at out celebrities to see that gay people can be successful in life, but out celebrities don't do much to help with our navigating a bully, or handling a crush on someone, or dodging questions about when we're going to get married, or deciding whether and when to come out. They don't help us with feeling *normal*.

Imagine if you'd had someone in your neighbourhood or family to look up to, who you could maybe talk to about life, who by just knowing they were there, you wouldn't feel so alone.

Coming out not only empowers us, it empowers those around us. By being out, we give a voice not only to ourselves, but to others, especially those who can't speak up for themselves. We become role models. We blaze a trail for those not yet out and all those who will come after. We become wayfinders for those who seek guidance. We give permission, both implicitly and explicitly, for others to become their best Selves. We act as Guides to the Unknown for those who can't see past the current moment. We motivate, teach, touch, and provide haven to those who are struggling. We reach others hearts and minds, all without saying a word.

Quite simply put, by living an out, normal existence, we inspire, offer hope, give comfort and respite to others, and in doing so, make the world a better place.

Human Rights — There's truth to the saying "there's strength in numbers". In our community, for example, the more gay people there are, the more important we become to society, business and governments. Look to a country where being out is more accepted than in yours. How did those societies get there? There was a normalization that happened over time – seeing gay characters in movies and on television, in people speaking out publicly about gay issues and human rights, and in public visibility (including Pride events and protests).

Understanding that gay people are everywhere changed societies and lawmaker's minds. By gay people coming out, standing up, and making our presence known, societies, governments and businesses begin to see how many of us there are, understand the political and economic power that the gay community has, and begin to change rules, laws and rights. The more gay people who are out in an organization or society at large, the more they have a voice in making laws, policies and procedures that further human rights for the gay community and, by extension, society at large.

As you self-reflect and take your own personal inventory on why you would like to come out.

Knowing Yourself

J: And so you came out at 35. When did you first know you were gay?

MW: I think I knew that I was only attracted to men at a really young age, maybe 5 or 6, but I wasn't aware that that made me "different" until I think I was maybe 10? That's when the other boys in school started teasing girls and talking about puberty and all the wrong ideas that kids get into their heads about where babies come from and all that.

J: Right.

MW: I think that's when I started to realize that I wasn't interested in what was happening to girls' bodies compared to the other boys in class and wondered what the fuss was about. But by the time I was 12 or 13, it was already totally clear to me that I was only interested in the male figure. Unfortunately, of course, that was the exact time when I entered high school, and an all-boys school at that.

J: An all-boys school? Oh my! Your parents were so good to you…

MW: Um, no…no, not really, but more on that later. Anyway, in school I started hearing new words that I had never heard before, some I immediately knew were derogatory or negative from the way they were spat out or used in a sentence, words like "sissy", "ah kua", and "bapok". Those words were hardly ever directed at me, but I saw other boys receive those labels, always unhappily, reluctantly, or defiantly. So just as I started to realize that I was attracted to males (and didn't know there was a word for that at the time), the behaviour of all the people around me started to indicate to me that this was not an acceptable thing to be. I suppose I considered myself somewhat lucky because I didn't appear to be very effeminate in behaviour.

J: Lucky to be at an all-boys school, I'd say, but continue …

MW: I saw that my friends who were more effeminate were bullied pretty mercilessly and I could not understand why. Why did the other boys behave as if my gentle friend was a THREAT to them? He was completely harmless and in fact a talented, kind and supportive person whom I thought was completely undeserving of the treatment he sometimes got from the other boys.

J: Yes, and these early emotional "disconnects" — when we feel one thing, but society tells us we should be feeling or doing something contrary to that — can be quite confusing in our emotional development. This is a common experience for many gay people.

MW: Yes, I didn't really know the word "gay" at that age, but I think I heard the word "homosexual" being used a couple of times. I think a lot of people my age will remember that the word "gay" used to refer to homosexuality was regarded back then as an alien, "Western" term, that didn't really translate into the context of our society. In fact, I think this partly explains why the idea of "being gay" has also sometimes been thought of as a "Western" phenomenon that either does not exist in Asian society, or is a foreign "disease" or "disorder" that was "imported" from the West.

J: Yeah, few Asian languages even have the vocabulary to discuss it. I mean, how do you talk about apples if people have never seen them and don't know how to describe them? Many Asian languages don't even have a word for gay, which is odd, considering homosexuality was openly practiced in many Asian societies throughout history. But yes, I think because of that lack of language and having to use "Western" terms, many countries across the Asian continent somehow see homosexuality as a social scourge brought upon them by foreigners.

MW: Right. I think because we didn't have language to identify and discuss gay people, they were sort of "invisible". There were just the life-long bachelors who lived together and supported each other. They weren't "gay," they weren't "homosexual," they were just the "odd uncles or aunties". When we started hearing words like "gay" and "lesbian" being used (and their direct translations in other languages), it felt like we had a word for it, but because they were

English words, the whole idea of it seemed foreign. And there was a further disconnect, that if people were "gay" they had to match some kind of stereotype, some combination of being flamboyant, promiscuous, and effeminate. Those were the Western images we were getting, what my father called "the American sitcom lifestyle that's invading our country."

J: With no laugh track, I'm guessing ….

MW: And so it kind of meant that the "odd uncles" couldn't be "gay" because they didn't match the stereotype. We didn't have gay characters on TV or in the movies for people to model, identify with or normalise, so being gay was a mystery. It was a Western thing. I think a lot of people from my parents' generation and older thought that way, not only in Singapore, but all across Asia.

J: But gay *was* an Asian thing — a very Asian thing — until the Western missionaries came and shut it all down!

MW: You mean the Cut Sleeve thing?

J: Yeah! But it wasn't only the Chinese with The Cut Sleeve — the Japanese, Thais, Indonesians, Indians — hell, it seems most of Asia had pretty open societies until the West came and screwed it all up with missionaries … and sitcoms.

Cultural Expectation in Confucian Societies

A Little Bit of History

Is homosexuality really a "Western" phenomenon and something completely foreign to Asian cultures? No, of course not. One important story in Chinese history is called the Passion of the Cut Sleeve. It is probably the most famous of all the Chinese stories of same-sex love, and tells of the romantic relationship between the Han dynasty Emperor Ai, and his male lover Dong Xian. The story goes that the emperor was so in love with Dong Xian that having awakened one morning to find his young lover still asleep, the emperor chose to cut off the sleeve of his robe in order to leave without disturbing Dong Xian.

For many centuries after, the term "cut-sleeve" was used as a term to refer to male homosexuality in China. This story gained notoriety in ancient China because it involved an emperor.

In contemporary Asia, it is still common to hear people condemn homosexuality as a recent import from the "decadent" West. However, many scholars note that this current anti-homosexual morality seems to have been derived from the West itself. In the late 19th and early 20th centuries, China suffered tremendous humiliation at the hands of Western and Japanese imperialists. The Chinese developed a sort of love-hate relationship with the West. On the one hand, progressive types saw Western science and technology as China's way to catch up and save her pride and civilization. On the other hand, in wanting to adopt Western technology and "scientific" thinking at the time, there was also a desire to adopt "modern" Western ideas in every aspect of life, including dressing, politics, and ultimately morals, which Christian missionaries had been trying to import into China for centuries by then.

These Christian missionaries and other Western moralists had hoped to bring China in line with their moral reasoning and values, leading to the stopping of feet-binding, prostitution, and the practice of having concubines. They had tremendous success in influencing Chinese society (both in China itself and among the diaspora) to gradually believe that these imported "modern" values and morals were somehow "native" to Chinese culture.

In a rather cruel twist of fate, after the "modernization" of China took place in the early 20th century, wars and political upheaval left the society isolated from the rest of the world for many decades. Separated from communities around the world, these outdated and misguided 19th century Western values and morals persisted — repeated from parents to children over and over — becoming ingrained in the culture as if they had been Chinese values all along.

In addition, with the adoption of Western thinking and language styles, Chinese sexual categories have changed. Instead of thinking of people in the traditional sense of having a potential range of sexual tendencies and preferences, it has become commonplace for Chinese people to think of sexuality in terms of strict Western-style categories and identities (homosexual vs heterosexual and nothing else).

In earlier times, the West saw the East as a "decadent" and "immoral" because homosexuality and sexuality in general was condoned and tolerated in Asian countries. Nowadays, Asian societies tend to look at the West as "depraved" and "unrooted" for being tolerant on LGBTQ+ rights and equality. The great irony is that this intolerance of homosexuality and sexual "deviance" that is so proudly branded as "Asian values" are in fact imported from the West, while the acceptance of homosexuality that Asians think of as "Western" immorality is much more typical of traditional Asian values.

J: The irony of all ironies, I suppose ...

MW: And it's not just China that was influenced by this. Cut Sleeve is a historical Chinese tale, but there are many others as well. In Japan, during the nearly 300-year Tokugawa period, homosexuality was very common and accepted. And in medieval Japan, parents placed their sons with Buddhist priests to educate and mentor them. Some would go into the priesthood and some would go on to be personal attendants and sexual partners for their Buddhist masters.

J: That makes my childhood seem really boring ...

M: I know.

J: But yeah, well beyond the Chinese diaspora, homosexuality, even transsexuality or "third gender", was practiced openly around the world in Polynesia, India, Thailand, Philippines, Indonesia, and among Native Americans and in the islands in the Pacific Rim.

MW: You just had to get the word "rim" in there, didn't you?

J: Ha-ha. You know me too well.

MW: For many of us who grew up in religious households, the issue of homosexuality and its place in religious texts is a deeply personal and complex one. It is a topic that has caused a great deal of pain, confusion, and division among families, friends, and religious communities.

J: I hear you. I went to Catholic school for 9 years. But sadly, there seem to be split forms of Christianity. Many in the church use the cover of religion as a moral judgment and a weapon against those they disapprove of. It seems to be about getting people to start acting, believing and behaving like you think they should behave.

MW: And that's just what the missionaries did throughout Asia in the whole Cut Sleeve thing.

J: Right. But there's another form of Christianity too. The teachings of Jesus preach compassion, understanding, forgiveness and inclusion of those different from us. I mean he supposedly hung out with a prostitute, Mary Magdalene, and saved her from death. "Let whoever is without sin cast the first stone," or something like that. They apparently became friends and hung out regularly after that.

MW: Religious leaders have been weaponizing religion for political and economic purposes throughout history. Ever heard of The Crusades?

J: Yes. 200 years, a million and a half dead. Started by a pope because Christians wanted "holy" land and would be absolved of sin if they killed Jews and Muslims to get it.

MW: And the Inquisition, hundreds of years of torturing and killing witches and heretics.

JR: And the Puritans coming to America, taking land and killing natives for "Divine Providence"; the centuries-long fight by American slave holders to keep slavery legal because it's okayed in the bible; and the "Christian" groups currently around the world fighting *against* diversity, inclusion and LGBTQ rights.

MW: Okay. I'm exhausted.

J: Me too. Should we pull over into that church over there and get some rest?

MW: Ha-ha.

:

MW: But getting back to the confluence of Western and Asian values and either accepting or rejecting sexuality, identity and gender, it's important to note that the basic reasons for intolerance are different in Asia and the West. In the West, most intolerance of homosexuality comes from religious and ethical reasons. In Asia, especially in Confucian societies, most objection comes from the fact that homosexuality may disrupt the natural cycle of reproduction and foundation of the family structure which is the fundamental unit of society.

J: Carrying on the family name is the main thing, yeah?

MW: Right. It used to be that a Chinese man could have a male lover that even his wife and family knew about, if he dutifully fulfilled his filial obligations to have a wife and bear (numerous) children. This was not only a way to build wealth — many hands were needed to work the family farm — but also to ensure the family lineage. As long as the family tree was continued, same-sex behaviour could be tolerated as an "indulgence" on the part of a man.

J: Indeed.

MW: But today, taking a wife shouldn't be a shield for sexual acceptance, nor a requirement to ensure family lineage. Today's medical science allows same-sex couples to have biological children of their own. Or, depending on the country, they can adopt. And with the way the world, planet and climate are changing, Asian cultures across the board might revaluate the importance of namesake in such an uncertain future.

J: I think that's happening now. With declining birth rates and marriage rates across Asia and much of the world, younger people seem to be evaluating and reprioritising the traditional values of family lineage. I think cultural mores are shifting.

MW: And they need to. We can all hope that countries throughout Asia will shed these imported, outdated ideas of sexuality and morality, and embrace a more tolerant, loving and inclusive view of society, allowing LGBTQ+ people the lives they desire and deserve.

J: Right. But changing what's accepted as "normal" as far as values goes, well, let's just say that redefining a new normal seems like a heavy lift.

MW: Yes, especially the values that Asian cultures hold dear.

J: For example?

MW: Start with filial piety — the respect, care and obedience to parents. In my culture you're expected not just to obey your parents, but to care for them and for your family as a whole. I remember my grandma used to proudly tell us stories of how my dad as the youngest child growing up poor would give up his food so that she wouldn't be upset that there wasn't enough for the rest of the family. It took me a long time to realize that she maybe was just telling that story to show how moved she was at my dad's gesture, and not that it's the way all children are expected to behave!

Thoughts on Confucian Culture and Filial Piety

What is Filial Piety? It is the respect, care and obedience to parents. The West has a lite version, known as "honour thy mother and thy father," but in many Asian societies, you must never go against your parents. You might disagree with them and have differing opinions, but they pretty much have the final say-so on things. That's how it's supposed to go, anyway. You're never really your own person until your parents die. You're programmed to please and uphold the general harmony of the family, which of course, depends on whatever your parents say. Confucian culture makes it easy for gay people to think they are "sparing" their parents the pain and discomfort of dealing with their sexuality by subordinating their needs (to be authentic and open) to that of their parents or family, because they think it's the "filial" thing to do. But if you choose to stay closeted so as not to upset your parents, are you really being filial and loving, or are you merely acting out of fear of the discomfort that might be caused by coming out? It's important to remember that we are not in control of what emotions other people feel. You are not responsible for how your parents (or anyone else) react to your coming out. Being filial doesn't simply mean making your parents stay as comfortable as possible. It can also mean being truthful with them and allowing them into your personal life if they wish to.

J: So, you grew up thinking you had to give up your own needs to get along?

MW: Yeah, that's what I thought being a good child was. I thought it was normal to subordinate myself for the comfort of others.

J: And speaking of normal, that's certainly a feeling that most young LGBTQ people wrestle with: Am I normal? Is same-sex attraction normal?

MW: It is. The disconnect between what one feels inside versus what a fearful and bigoted society tells them can be confusing, possibly even devastating. And it's sad that there is a disconnect at all because the answer to "Is being gay normal?" is a resounding YES!

You Are Normal!

Birds do it, Bees do it

There's an argument often made by anti-LGBTQ crusaders that same-sex relations – pairing, bonding, mating and sex – are somehow unnatural acts; however, nothing could be further from the truth. Science has for many years been studying same-sex pairings throughout the animal kingdom and has found homosexuality across all classes: in mammals, birds, insects, reptiles, amphibians, fish and other invertebrates. In fact, no species has been found in which homosexual behaviour has not been shown to exist, except for species that never have sex at all, such as sea urchins or aphids. Moreover, a part of the animal kingdom is hermaphroditic; that is to say, truly bisexual. For them, homosexuality is not an issue.

Did you know...

Up to 90% of giraffe sex is male on male. (Talk about some serious necking!) It is extremely common for two male giraffes to caress and court each other, leading up to mounting and climax. In fact, such interactions between males have been found to be far more frequent than heterosexual coupling.

Both male and female Asian elephants engage in homosexual activity, with about 45% of sexual encounters being as such. Male elephants of this and other species often live away from the herd, and it is common for an older male to take one or two younger "companion" males to live, travel and have sex with.

Bottlenose dolphins of both genders regularly engage in homosexual sex, using it as a social bonding mechanism. In fact, in confrontations between flocks of bottlenose dolphins and Atlantic spotted dolphins, males will often engage in group sex rather than in combat. 10% of male sheep are exclusively homosexual and will only mount males even in the presence of oestrous ewes, and up to 20% of all sheep are bisexual. In several sheep species in the wild (bighorn, thinhorn, Asian mouflons, urials), both genders have been observed having homosexual sex in groups of up to 10, which scientists call "huddles." For farmers breeding domestic sheep, the Merck Manual of Veterinary Medicine considers homosexuality among sheep as such a routine occurrence that it's an issue to be dealt with in animal husbandry.

And the list goes on and on. Whether you're a bird, bat, bison, bonobo, bedbug, or Bob from the Boardroom, your homosexuality is completely normal and natural. Among the animals, sexuality does not affect social dynamics and functioning, or make them vulnerable to attack, or impede the continuance of the species. It just is what it is: A normal part of existence. Period.

If you think the comparison between animals and humans is silly, think again. In 2003, the United States Supreme Court heard the case of Lawrence v. Texas, in which two men were found having sex in their apartment and were arrested. Documents submitted to the court by the American Psychiatric Association and other groups argued that homosexuality was not a criminal act, citing natural homosexuality in animals as their basis of fact. The court listened. The ruling in that case struck down the existing sodomy laws in 14 U.S. states as unconstitutional.

So, dear reader, when you hear the old trope that homosexuality is not "normal," remind yourself that, as a fully-fledged member of this grand kingdom we call the Natural World, you are as normal as all the other animals in the world.

MW: I wish kids could learn that earlier, that they're normal. There can be so much trauma for us while learning that.

J: So true. And coming to terms with yourself and understanding and accepting who you really are is the first step in coming out.

MW: Yes, it is. But it's so difficult a lot of the time getting to that point. First, from the minute you even think you're gay it can make you feel disconnected from the greater society, make you feel "less than."

J: Yes, you can feel like you're an outcast simply for the way you were created. That can have devastating effects for many.

MW: And all the microaggressions we face, people saying things like "That's so gay", or "Wow, isn't she/he hot?", or hearing gay jokes and put downs, it's a lot to cope with as a kid.

J: As adults too. People asking questions like, "Why don't you have a girl/boyfriend?" or "When are you going to get married?" or "Do you have any kids? Oh, why not?" … . If we can't be totally honest, questions like these can put us on the defensive when we shouldn't be

MW: Yes, all these experiences can throw us into self-doubt, diminish our sense of self-worth, push us deeper into the closet, and inflict serious shame and guilt, even to the point of suicide.

J: Which is why it's *so important* for LGBT people to know they're normal. If you're questioning your sexuality or gender identity, it's normal. If you're attracted to the same sex or have same-sex fantasies, it's normal. If you're bisexual, asexual, pansexual or whatever, you're normal. You might be different from the next person, but you're normal. Because for human sexuality, there is no normal. There's only a range of differences. The diversity among us is what's normal. Alfred Kinsey published the science on that in 1948.

MW: Right, and it's coming to that realization of normal that's the first step to true authenticity. Reconciling the past is the first step to coming out.

Reader Reflection

As a gay person, you may have experienced the painful struggle of denying your own sexuality. Denying your sexuality can take many forms, from keeping your feelings hidden from friends and family to actively pretending to be something you are not. Take a moment and think about the first time you remember clearly having to deny your sexuality or feel embarrassed by it. For example, hearing homophobic jokes, someone calling you gay, finding your toys or pornography, starting rumours about you, or actually suffering physical or sexual abuse.

What was the situation like and how did it make you feel?

How would you have developed if these hadn't happened, or if your sexuality didn't matter to anyone?

The effects of denying your sexuality can be long-lasting and profound. Hiding your true self can damage your self-esteem and confidence, create anxiety and depression, and make it difficult to form intimate relationships. It's important to recognize that our sexuality is a fundamental aspect of our identity, and we should never feel ashamed or guilty for expressing ourselves. Having a picture of how we might develop without fear or judgment should serve to reinforce this idea. We should strive to create a world where everyone can feel safe and comfortable expressing their true selves. Such is the work (and benefit) of coming out.

MW: As I was saying, reconciling the past is the first step toward coming out and living an authentic life.

J: Yes, and that reconciliation is actually a letting go of the old self. It's recognizing the fear that we've held for so long. The fear of rejection, of humiliation, of embarrassment, of loneliness, of losing friends, of losing jobs, of destroying social bonds, of upsetting parents, of bringing disappointment or disgrace to the family. Most of all, the fear of not being loved for who we truly are.

MW: Fear can be crippling. It hinders so much of our lives, and yet we live with it, learn to accept it, even embrace it, as a survival mode.

J: But it's critical to let that fear go in order to open ourselves to love.

MW: Yes, it is. But that's much easier said than done.

J: Spoil sport ...

MW: It takes work and commitment, but also a clear understanding of what love and fear are, and how they shape our thoughts and actions.

Some Thoughts on Fear and Love

Let's take a minute to think about two powerful feelings that shape our actions as humans: love and fear. These emotions are like opposites, similar to how day and night are different but together make up our lives. Love often brings positive feelings like joy and happiness, while fear usually brings negative feelings like worry and stress. Both love and fear are like the roots of our emotions, influencing how we think, act, and react to the world around us.

Love is like a positive force that brings people closer and makes strong connections between us. It inspires us to care for others, be kind, and connect with people. Love comes in many forms, like the love you feel for your romantic partner, your family, your friends, or even for yourself. It encourages us to be understanding, compassionate, and helpful to others. Love also helps us feel like we belong and have a purpose in the world.

True love is when you can be completely honest and open with someone, knowing they care about you and won't judge you. Sometimes, acts of love might not feel comfortable or easy. For example, helping a family member who is struggling with a problem might mean setting boundaries or having a difficult conversation. It can be tough and emotional, but it's a loving action that can make things better in the end. Similarly, coming out as LGBTQ+ to your family and friends might be challenging and scary, but it's a way of being true to yourself and deepening your connections with others. Love is what makes life beautiful and meaningful.

Now, let's talk about fear. Fear is like a negative force that kicks in when we sense danger. It's a natural reaction that helps us survive in threatening situations. But sometimes, fear can hold us back and make us feel unsure or scared about things. It can come from past experiences, not knowing what's going to happen, or facing the unknown. Fear can make us defensive and react with anger or aggression. It can also make us want to be alone to protect ourselves, and it can stop us from taking risks, going after our dreams, and living life to the fullest.

When it comes to deciding whether or not to come out, both love and fear play important roles. Fear can be a major part of it because you might worry about how others will react or if you'll face discrimination or judgement. You may also feel responsible for causing hurt feelings in your loved ones. It's natural to feel anxious about these things, and at times the anxiety can be overwhelming.

But love is just as important in this decision. Loving and accepting yourself are crucial steps in embracing your true identity and having the courage to be open about it. When you truly love yourself, you recognize your own worth and understand that you deserve to be your authentic self. Wanting to deepen your relationships, live honestly, and be truthful with people all come from a place of love.

Let's try a little thought experiment. Imagine someone says they won't come out because they don't want to hurt their family. What do you think drives this decision - love or fear?

You might think, "I care about my family, so not coming out to avoid upsetting them is a loving thing to do." But let's dig deeper. Could it be that you're not coming out because you're afraid of how people will react or how your family might change? In that case, it's not really about love; it's more about fear.

Now, let's flip the scenario. What if coming out to your family and friends strengthened your bonds? What if it brought you all closer together? Imagine not having to hide or lie anymore, which could improve your relationships and your ability to connect with others. What if being honest and true to yourself boosted your self-esteem? What if you found out that people love and accept you for who you are, not who they thought you were?

Think about it from your loved ones' perspective. If you came out and they reacted with concern, thinking your life might be tough, it might seem like they're doing it out of love to protect you. But, in reality, they might be acting out of fear - fear of the unknown, fear of difficulties you might face, or other worries. If this happens, remember that their reaction comes from fear, and the best way to counter it is with love. Show them empathy, understanding, and positivity to help them move past their fears.

Remember, true love means being open, honest, and authentic, even when it's scary or uncomfortable. By doing so, you're rejecting fear and showing your family that you truly care about them. Coming out might involve facing potential negativity and uncertainty, but you do it in the name of love. It's about strengthening your connections with loved ones, living authentically, and facing the world without fear.

J: Yes, there's a fine line between love and fear. They're often difficult to separate.

MW: But when you do, it's easier to view the world that way. Unless you're being chased by a bear, fear is usually imaginary.

J: That bears repeating . . .

MW: Ugh. But seriously, when faced with an unsettling situation, we think of all the bad things that might happen. That's fear. Rather than looking for the potential good that may come, which is love. And in looking at a situation and reacting to it, here's always a choice. You have to ask yourself, "What's the most loving thing I can do here?" It takes work to see things that way, but I find it always ends in a good result. Love creates more love.

J: And fear creates more fear. Just as in the dreaded "loop".

MW: Yes, the anxiety loop, where fear breeds stress, and that stress breeds more fear, and it goes on and on and can take a serious toll on us.

J: Yeah, I don't think most people know about that, but it's a bear - haha, see what I did there?

MW: Again, ugh.

J: But that negative feedback loop we create can bring on anxiety, depression, persistent feelings of guilt, even the inability to form and maintain close relationships.

Fear and the Anxiety Loop

There is a construct in psychology known as the anxiety loop. Let's look at how this works around keeping a secret. Keeping secrets can cause stress. The bigger the secret, the more the stress. Hiding our sexuality/true self is a very big secret, and so causes a lot of stress, guilt and shame. And because we *have* this secret, we need to *keep* it secret. This, too, causes stress and anxiety and creates a "secrecy spiral." It works like this: Every time we encounter a situation where our sexuality is an issue, we think about the secret we have, which creates stress. And when the secret enters our minds, we try to repress it, which causes more stress.

There is further anxiety in making sure it stays a secret, the fear that no one finds out about it. When we're in the closet, we end up putting our secret under constant surveillance to make sure it stays well-hidden. But inevitably, the secret will re-emerge in our minds — often many times a day (stress) — causing us to try to repress it (stress) — and making sure we keep it secret from others (even more stress).

Coming out eliminates what for most of us is our deepest and longest held secret. It eliminates the constant fear of being "found out," and all the stress, guilt and shame that goes along with it. Nearly everyone who comes out reports feelings of freedom, of honesty, of a better sense of Self. These feelings of "lightness" and "relief" come from shedding the mental and emotional weight of keeping the secret buried, and constantly worrying whether it will be somehow revealed.

J: When you came out, how long did you think about it before you finally told somebody?

MW: How long was the Ming Dynasty? No, seriously, I came out to a friend first, but I'd thought about it for about a year before I told him.

J: Was it a year because it took that long to work up the nerve?

MW: Yes, to make sure I really wanted to come out, and that I was ready and knew who I was. There was a LOT of reading, research and self-reflection in that process. A lot of questioning, a lot of doubt. As I learned later, I was just working through the stages of coming out.

J: Oh, the stages. Yes. Moving through the various emotional phases of coming to terms with who we are. We all go through them. Some people move through them quickly, others take longer, but the stages are always there, both for us coming out to ourselves and for those we come out to.

MW: I don't think many people are aware of the process as it's happening, that they're actually moving stages. I know I didn't.

J: Me neither. But when you look at it, it makes sense. And awareness or not, I think everyone knows when they've reached the final stage, that stage of *acceptance*, of knowing who we really are, being certain, and coming to terms with ourselves.

MW: I know I sure did. It took some time, but eventually I arrived at a loving place with myself — still nervous and a bit unsure — but understanding who I was and that that wasn't going to change. I finally made a plan to come out to my friend and then did it. Turns out he was gay too and came out to me at the same time. We both were incredibly happy and relieved. It was a very special moment.

The Stages of Grief (And of Coming Out)

We've said it before and will say it again a thousand times, coming out is a *process*. It's a process we do internally over time to fully accept ourselves, a process we do with others each time we let them know who we truly are, and a process others go through to accept us when we come out to them.

An important part of the coming out process – for us and for those we come out to – is the need to "unlearn" the LGBTQ myths and stereotypes we've heard all our lives and have come to believe are true. We are usually reluctant to come out because of uncertainty in ourselves and uncertainty of how others will react to us coming out. Both these fears are usually based on a preconceived notion of what gay people are like – what they look like, how they act, what they can and can't do, etc. These stereotypes are usually based on what is portrayed in the media and/or believed by our families and friends. So, a major task in us accepting us and of others accepting us, is to "unlearn" those stereotypes, to release them from our psyches and emotionally "bury" them.

While this burial/acceptance process moves us closer to our true selves, it is also rife with loss – the loss of imagined/hoped-for heterosexuality, the loss of heteronormative societal expectations, the loss of not fulfilling our parent's dreams of a traditional wedding and subsequent grandchildren, the loss of the emotional shelter being in the closet provides, the loss of our inauthentic selves – the people we pretended to be all these years. And just as with other losses in life – loved ones, relationships, pets, a job – getting over them involves a certain amount of grieving.

Dr. Elizabeth Kubler Ross, a Swiss-American psychiatrist and expert on near-death studies, first outlined the stages of grief associated with death and loss in her ground-breaking book, *On Death and Dying* (1969). These stages of grief have been recognized and accepted internationally for not only death, but for emotional losses of all kinds, including the process of coming out.

The stages are: Denial – Anger – Bargaining – Depression – Acceptance. The examples in parentheses below are as if you had a loved one just about to die.

Denial — (*They'll pull through this, I'm sure. It'll all be okay*).

Anger — (*The doctors aren't doing enough!! Why aren't they working harder? Why is God making us suffer like this?!!*)

Bargaining — (*If you let him/her live, I'll give the rest of my life to helping people.*)

Depression — (*Oh, s/he's going to die. I feel so lost, helpless, and empty…*)

Acceptance — (*You were the love of my life. I hope you're at peace. I don't know how I'm going to carry on.*)

The examples above are about death, but the stages of grief apply to all kinds of loss and/or personal transformation, including leaving our closeted selves behind when we come out.

MW: You've lost loved ones, haven't you?

J: Yes, my father, three siblings, and several friends. Most happened when I was much younger.

MW: And did you go through the Stages of Grief then?

J: Well, I didn't know I was going through them while it was happening, but yes, I did. And I think we do with every loss, whether it's a death, a relationship ending, the loss of a job or, in the case of closeted people, the loss of an identity we were holding onto to be loved and accepted by others.

MW: That's an important point: That there is definitely a grieving process to coming out, to losing that closeted persona, the person we pretended for so long to be. We build that "cover" personality to fit in, to be someone we think others will accept and respect. And it usually serves us very well. It helps us survive day to day. But when we come out, we say goodbye to that "cover" because we no longer need it. We bury it, so to speak.

J: Right. And that's loss. That's grief. That's losing a trusted friend we've held very close to us for a very long time. So it's not hard to see how the stages of grief also become the stages of coming out, whether we're coming out to ourselves or to other people.

Below are the Stages of Grief modified as the Stages for Coming Out to Ourselves. The examples in parentheses might be typical of what someone would think or feel while in that stage. It's important to understand that the stages aren't linear, that is, we don't work through one, then move onto the next. We may experience two or more stages simultaneously.

The Stages of Grief for Coming Out to Ourselves

Denial – (*I can't be gay. I don't fit the stereotype. I don't know any gay people. I've never had sex with a guy/girl, so I can't be gay. This is just a phase I'm going through.*)

Anger – (*This isn't fair. Why do I have to be gay? Why can't I be normal? I don't even like gay people.*)

Bargaining – (*Maybe if I date the opposite sex, I'll grow out of this. My friends and family will be okay with things if I just don't talk about it. Maybe I can just get married and keep my urges under control.*)

Depression – (*Everyone is going to hate me. I'm going to bring shame on my family. My life is going to be awful.*)

Acceptance – (*I'm gay. I am who I am. And I'm much more than my sexuality. I can achieve great things. I want loving, mutually rewarding relationships.*)

J: When you came out did you feel completely ready?

MW: No, like I said, I was still nervous and a bit uncertain, working through a few of the stages at once, I suppose. But I had gotten to that place of acceptance. I knew that I was ready, that I wasn't going to change, and that I just am who I am. I reached a place where I was okay with me and I wanted others to be okay with me too. It was time.

J: Right. And it's hard sometimes for people we come out to. They go through stages of grief too, some quickly, others not so much.

MW: Well, it's an emotional thing.

J: True, and the people we come out to often need to work through the same emotions that WE had to work through before deciding to come out. Just as coming out is a process for us, it's a process for them too.

MW: Yes, that's certainly been my experience. My friends and sister accepted the news pretty much immediately. But my parents, even years later, are still working through things. They're not yet at the acceptance phase.

J: So, what do you tell someone about coming out when their parents might not be accepting?

MW: I think it helps to remember that coming out to parents is something you do out of love, but you also do it for yourself. It's your acknowledgement of self-acceptance and telling others that you're okay with that. If your parents aren't accepting at first, at least you have put it out there for them to work on. You'll have tried to honour them by sharing your most authentic self with them. You'll also have provided them a chance to grow, to be more understanding and accepting, and to better know you.

J: Important points ...

MW: But if you never come out to them, you'll never give them the chance to know you completely. You'll go on keeping secrets and harbouring the emotional distance that comes with that. Acceptance — for families and friends — is oftentimes a process. People need to work through the stages of grief to get to an emotional place of acceptance. And different people move at different paces.

You might find that people need some time to accept you as you are. They may need to work through the stages and feel all the emotions that go along with them before they can reach the acceptance stage. Remember that they are saying goodbye to something they thought was true. They may be confused at first. Be patient and supportive. It's big news for both of you.

The Stages of Grief for Those We Come Out To

Below are the Stages of Grief as they might be experienced by an unsuspecting parent, friend or loved one:

Denial – *You can't be gay. No child/friend of mine is gay. I don't want to hear about it. You just haven't found the right person yet.*

Anger – *How could you do this to our family? What did we do wrong? What will our friends think? Whatever you do, don't tell anyone else. You're screwing your life up.*

Bargaining – *This is just a phase; you'll grow out of it. We'll find a doctor or therapist for you. Why don't we find a date for you? Why would you choose to be gay? I don't ever want to meet anyone you're with. Are you still gay?*

Depression – *You are going to have a very difficult life. You're going to get fired from your job. We'll never have grandkids. The family name will not be passed along. We don't know who you are anymore.*

Acceptance – *Thank you for telling me. I appreciate your honesty. We want you to be happy and we're here for you.*

Just as it may not have been easy for you to come out to yourself or others, it is not always easy for others to have someone come out to them. It's helpful to remember that coming out is an emotional process of burying the old in order to embrace the new. The path to authenticity and self-acceptance is travelled in stages rather than all at once. When coming out, people may have many questions for you or they may be silent and need time to digest the information. Either way, be patient and treat them in a kind, loving and supportive manner.

J: Can I just say something?

MW: Is it that you won the lottery?

JR: Yes, and we're moving to Bora Bora immediately. You'll need to pack tonight.

MW: Well, I ...

MW: No, what I wanted to say is that while I agree that it's important to come out for one's self, I also think we do it for others. Sharing our deepest and most authentic selves with others breaks down the barriers between us. It can bond us together. Our closest friends are those we share the most and are the most honest with. We don't keep secrets from them. And that candour and intimacy is what makes them our closest friends.

MW: Do you want to know a secret?

J: Oooh, okay! Yes!

MW: Don't get excited. It's not really a secret.

J: Awww... are you going to tell me you love me?

MW: Well, okay. But also, we need to stop on the way home. We're out of ice cream.

J: Was that your plan? To keep us talking and driving around until we get to the ice cream store?

MW: Well, you know, whether it's vacation, a career, coming out, or dessert, you've got to have a plan!

Making a Plan

Coming out is a huge event, one with countless rewards, but also possible risks. It is, without a doubt, one of the most important things you will ever do for yourself. And while there is no right or wrong way to come out — how it is best done is up to the person coming out – there are some things to consider that can make the process easier for you and those you come out to. Let's look at a few of them.

1. **Come out at your own pace, in your own way, and when you are ready.**

   Coming out is a process, one you'll repeat with each person you come out to. It is a difficult and possibly risky thing to do. You must make sure that YOU"RE ready, and that you're coming out for YOU, not because other people have come out, or because you feel pressured by someone to do it. When you're ready to come out, you'll know it. There will still be a LOT of fear to deal with before you finally "have the talk", but you'll definitely know when it's time.

2. **Be sure you're comfortable with your sexuality / identity before coming out.**

   As we've said, it's important that you know you're ready to come out. It's also important that you know who you are and why you want to come out. This seems like a silly and obvious thing to say, but once you've come out of the closet, there's no going back in. So, an important part of the coming out process is first coming out to yourself, being comfortable with your sexuality/identity and "owning" it, and being able to put that into words to share with others.

Questions that might help you get to know this better are: When did you first know you were LGBTQ? Have you ever had to deny your sexuality or felt embarrassed by it? What would your life be like if your sexuality wasn't an issue? Answering these and going through thoughts and memories of real and imagined encounters can help to reinforce our sexual identities.

3. Make a plan.

Such an important life event is best managed with a plan. Your coming out plan should include as many details of who, what, why, when, where, and how as possible. You may find it helpful to write everything down and/or use the checklist at the end of this book.

Who – Deciding who to (or not to) come out to is an important decision. It is usually best to choose a trusted, supportive person, someone who can keep your news a secret if you ask them to. A good place to start might be with a close friend, someone who has a lot of gay friends, or someone who is already gay. In deciding about coming out to family, you may want to start off with a sibling because it might be easier for them to understand differences in sexuality/identity. You could also choose to tell one parent first and then use that parent's help to tell the other. If deciding whether to come out at work, it is important to remember that many workplaces do not offer protections for LGBTQ people. But even if they do, it's important to be aware that employees gossip, and managers can discriminate in a way that isn't obviously based on your sexuality. Be it friend, family or workplace, if there is someone you want to come out to, but are not sure if that person would be receptive, it can be helpful to discuss LGBTQ topics first, just to get a feel for their reaction. "I heard Taiwan made gay marriage legal. What do you think about that?" or "They're debating the 377A law in Singapore.

Have you heard about that?" or "I just read an article about same sex couples adopting kids. What do you think?" or "I heard Kal Penn is gay". Introducing topics such as these can "break the ice" and, based on a person's reaction, help you understand their thoughts and feelings *before* you come out to them.

When – Simply put, do it when you're ready. But more specifically, plan to come out to someone when you're not rushed, when you both have time to discuss and process the news. It is also important to be in a good state of mind. You don't want to come out when you're angry, frustrated, tired, or otherwise distracted. Finally, it is not advised to come out at someone else's celebration, such as a birthday, wedding or graduation; rather, it's best to come out at a time when your news can be the sole focus of the event.

Where – There are several things to think about when deciding where to deliver the big news. Many people choose a private place to avoid the commotion and distractions that can happen in public places, and to avoid any possible public embarrassment from a negative reaction by those we come out to. Privacy has advantages because a quiet setting can be more intimate for a personal discussion. On the other hand, if coming out to someone may cause a physical threat or danger, a public place is most likely the best option for you.

Why – We spoke about this above, but the main "why" is because you are ready to be you, and to tell the world just who you are. You don't *need* a reason to come out. But some reasons might be because you are proud and comfortable with yourself as a person; because you feel uncomfortable keeping your sexuality suppressed; because you want to meet others who share your sexuality and be a part of the LGBTQ community and a part of its larger history; because you are (or want to be) in a relationship and want to introduce people to your partner. Again, no one needs a reason to come out, but as part of the planning process, it's helpful for us to know exactly why we're doing it.

How – There are many ways to come out. Some celebrities have come out publicly on TV talk shows, some in interviews, some have made announcement videos on YouTube. But for most of us, coming out is a quieter, more intimate affair. Spend some time visualizing the scene in your mind and practicing what you're going to say. It's not uncommon to be all set to tell someone but get so nervous in the moment that you have to put it off until later. If you know what you want to say, but cannot find the strength to say it, you might find it helpful to write that person a letter. Some people find it easiest to come out on social media, as there is no immediate discussion or questions to answer. But it's important to remember that social media can be shared/forwarded, possibly to people and places you don't want it to go. Voicemails and texts are other options, as are video calls, which can allow you to hang up if the conversation turns badly. Perhaps the simplest approach is to schedule a special time in a place with no distractions to share your exciting news.

What – Once you know who you're going to tell and where you're going to tell them, you'll need to decide *what* you're going to tell them. Your choice of words is a personal matter, of course, but it is important to choose your words with love. Remember that as difficult as it is for you to come out, it may be just as difficult for those you come out to. People have seen you a certain way and you're telling them you're not who they thought you were. It might be difficult for them to understand or accept at first. It's also possible they may not know any gay people or not know how to talk about this issue. Allow the other person space and time to process the information. Often, people want to say something supportive but don't know how to respond. They may be silent for a while. That's okay. It's up to you to lead the conversation, make a safe space for discussion, and be prepared for whatever response you might get. This does not mean you have to answer every question you are asked, especially personal/sexual ones. It's perfectly fine to say, "I'm not comfortable talking about that right now, but maybe we can in the future."

4. Celebrate!

While coming out is a process that repeats itself over and over throughout our lives, coming out the first few times is a milestone and should be celebrated! You have worked hard, planned well and had the courage to show your authentic self to the world, to stand up and be counted for who you are. Do something nice for yourself! Have a spa day! Go have dinner at a fancy restaurant! Throw yourself a Coming Out Party! Whatever you do, love yourself!

J: Did you do something to celebrate when you came out to your parents?

MW: My initial thing was just to decompress. I appeared calm during the conversation, but was really nervous on the inside, as we all are when coming out. So I just wanted to stop shaking

J: Right, ha-ha.

MW: But I did pour a big glass of wine and video-called my sis, who I was already out to. We had a really long, intimate and uplifting chat. It was wonderful. How about you?

J: Oh, I haven't *stopped* celebrating. You know I love a good party ...

MW: Yeah, I've been meaning to talk to you about that...

J: Anyway ...ha-ha. Whatever you do, it's important to find some time and some way to congratulate yourself for coming to terms with yourself, working through the stages of coming out, making a plan and gathering the courage to execute it, and for sharing the news about your authentic self with people in a patient and loving way.

MW: It's a life-changing event! And it should be celebrated! Cheers!

Coming Out Asian Planning Template

You can use the template below to formulate a detailed plan for coming out.

Who to Come Out to: — It's important to first come out to someone you trust and who is supportive. That person should also be able to keep the information confidential if you request it. Use the column on the right when deciding who to come out to first.

List 5 people you want to come out to.

Rank these individuals in order of trust, support and confidentiality.

1. _____   1. _____

2. _____   2. _____

3. _____   3. _____

4. _____   4. _____

5. _____   5. _____

When to Come Out: — Choose a time when you have enough time for a discussion, are in a good state of mind, are sure there won't be any distractions or negative emotions, and are sure that YOU will be the primary focus.

Where to Come Out: — Choose a private place to avoid distractions and potential embarrassment. And always consider your physical safety. If there's a threat or danger, a public place might be a safer option.

Why Come Out: — Reflect on your personal reasons for coming out, such as being proud and comfortable with yourself, feeling uncomfortable keeping your sexuality suppressed. wanting to connect with the LGBTQ community and its history, introducing your partner to others, or just wanting to share your true and authentic self with others.

How to Come Out — Visualize the scene and practice what you want to say. It could be an in-person conversation, a written letter, on social media, or a voicemail, text or video call:

What to Say — Choose your words with love and understanding. Recognize that coming out may be difficult for both you and the person you're telling, so allow the other person space and time to process the information, and be prepared for different reactions.

(Turn to next page)

Person 1

Who _____

When _____

Where _____

What to Say _____

_____

_____

_____

_____

_____

_____

Anticipated problems _____

_____

_____

_____

How I'm going to celebrate _____

_____

_____

Person 2

Who _____

When _____

Where _____

What to Say _____

_____

_____

_____

_____

_____

_____

Anticipated problems _____

_____

_____

_____

How I'm going to celebrate _____

_____

_____

Person 3

Who _____

When _____

Where _____

What to Say _____

_____

_____

_____

_____

_____

Anticipated problems _____

_____

_____

_____

How I'm going to celebrate _____

_____

_____

Person 4

Who _____

When _____

Where _____

What to Say _____

_____

_____

_____

_____

_____

_____

Anticipated problems _____

_____

_____

_____

How I'm going to celebrate _____

_____

_____

Person 5

Who _____

When _____

Where _____

What to Say _____

_____

_____

_____

_____

_____

Anticipated problems _____

_____

_____

_____

How I'm going to celebrate _____

_____

_____

A Few Words from Us

Congratulations on coming this far in your journey. Hopefully you have learned something about yourself and about the process of coming out, and are now better equipped to share your true self with the world when the time is right.

Coming out of the closet is a life-changing experience that can bring a lot of emotions. First and foremost, it's important to expect a sense of relief. Keeping such a significant aspect of your life hidden can be emotionally exhausting. And the longer you have, the more exhausting it can be. Coming out can provide a sense of freedom, dignity and authenticity. It's common to feel a sense of empowerment and self-confidence after you share your truth, as you no longer have to hide who you are from those around you.

There are times, however, that we experience negative reactions from those around us. Unfortunately, there is still a lot of stigma surrounding the LGBTQ+ community, and not everyone may be accepting of your identity. Even so, it's important to remember that you are valid and worthy of love and acceptance, regardless of the reactions of others.

Overall, coming out of the closet is a profoundly liberating experience. By being true to yourself and living authentically, you can find a sense of peace and fulfilment that can help you lead a happy and fulfilling life. Remember, you are not alone, and there is a whole community of people who are here to support and love you for who you are.

As you continue your journey, it's important to remember that there are resources available to help you navigate challenges that may arise, such as LGBTQ+ support groups and advocacy organizations. You can usually find resources online or in your community.

And we're available at www.ComingOutAsian.com. We invite you to send us a note on our website, set up an individual chat session or register for one of our in-depth workshops.
We wish you strength, peace, joy and love in your journey!

All the best to you,

John & Mun Wye

About the Authors

John and Mun Wye met in Florida in 2014, fell in love on their third date and have been together since. As a cross-cultural couple, their story has been one of navigating the complex and often challenging waters of inter-cultural norms, world views, and the expectations so prevalent in Asian families and society. It has been a constant journey toward growing as individuals and as a couple, and this has inspired them to help others, in particular, those from Asian backgrounds who may be on different stages of the same journey.

Follow them on Instagram and Facebook @comingoutasian, or on their website www.comingoutasian.com.

Made in the USA
Monee, IL
20 November 2023

46890277R10049